# CREATING MEMORABLE & DYNAMIC CHARACTERS

*Developing Personalities Readers Will Identify With and Believe In*

Joy A. Burke

Story Consultant & Developmental Editor

**Creating Memorable & Dynamic Characters**
*Developing Personalities Readers Will Identify With
and Believe In*

www.hahaink.com

ISBN-13: 978-1511640886

Cover design by Joy A. Burke.
Photo from Pixaby.com under CC License CC0 1.0 Universal

Printed in the United States of America

# Table of Contents

# Introduction

The day I finished reading *The Hobbit,* I set the book down, looked across the field behind my house, and wanted nothing more than to pack my bag with bread, cheese, and a hanky and set off on my own adventure. Bilbo Baggins, Thorin and Company, and all the other characters thereafter in Middle Earth have stayed with me

There are some characters that enter our lives either through reading or movies that tend to stick with us for years.

As writers, we all want our characters to be memorable, to go down as the next Elisabeth Bennett or Hannibal Lector – depending on what you write.

So how do we write such characters?

First, let's take a look at what makes some of the most memorable characters, memorable.

As we go through each section of this book, I hope you will take the time to consider the various ideas discussed and work through the exercises by creating a new character, or working with one you are developing. It's a great opportunity to see how characters are created and discover that they're already lurking in the fog of our imaginations!

# Creating Memorable & Dynamic Characters

Draw your readers in by learning the fundamentals of creating
fiction and non-fiction that hooks!

## *Haha! Ink!*
## *Creative Studios*

## Joy A. Burke

Story Consultant & Developmental Editor

# What Makes Characters Memorable

**Elisabeth Bennett** – *Pride and Prejudice*

Elisabeth Bennett is believed to be one of the most beloved characters in English literature. Her independent nature and thinking, her obvious intelligence, as well as her inability to refrain from saying what's on her mind has endeared her to new and veteran readers.

Jane Austen created a strong and remarkable character in Elizabeth Bennett. The fact that she is so unlike her contemporaries is likely one of the main reasons she is so memorable to us. She is also a wonderful mix of stubborn and compassionate. In an era where women were subject to men, expected to behave a certain way, and generally bow to society's rules and regulations, Elizabeth Bennett embodies the woman all others wish they could be. Even today, when so many do not have a voice or are simply not comfortable with who they are, Elizabeth Bennett continues to be an example of a strong yet gentle heroine.

This young woman is content to be who she is, where she is and voices her opinion if she's not. If she can be proactive to change her circumstances she will, if not she simply moves on. It's a lesson I'm sure we'd all love to learn.

The only thing that leaves you wondering about her, is if she was the one who was proud or prejudiced.

**Hannibal Lecter** – Silence of the Lambs

Such an evil character in so many people's eyes.

It's true, Hannibal Lecter is a disturbed character – but brilliant nonetheless. He provides insight to an ongoing investigation no other can and it is his information that ultimately allows agent Starling to apprehend the murderer.

Hannibal Lecter is a complex character.

On the one hand, he is deranged and dangerous. On the other, he is brilliant and kind. Agent Starling reaches out, exposes her deepest fears, and is able to connect with him and as a result, he opens up just enough to show us he is not completely lost.

He helps agent Starling discover the strength she has as an agent and officer. He is true to his word, provides more than she asked for, and in fact calls to congratulate her on her day of graduation. Hannibal Lecter has his own sense of justice and knowing how he and Starling were both treated by the hospital physiatrist, he asserts his revenge against him.

Hannibal Lecter is a creepy and disturbing character. But unforgettable. He's not the movie's primary villain since he's aiding the FBI, but he's certainly not the hero.

No matter what role he serves, he stays in your mind for his heinous acts and as a key piece to the puzzle, and if you are anything like me, you wonder if there is a Hannibal Lector anywhere on the street you're walking.

**Robert de Bruce** – Braveheart

Robert de Bruce is, for me, one of the most sympathetic characters in movie history.

He is a memorable character for me because he believes in what William Wallace is fighting for and wants to join him, but has familial allegiance to his oppressive father, and clan allegiance to the other clan leaders. As a young man and future king, he is torn between his heart and what he knows deep down to be the correct path, and his obligations and the pressures of the other more experienced leaders around him.

In the end, we know what happens and he is true to his heart but not without a cost. But when I watch this drama play out for him, it always feels like the story of us. Who of us hasn't faced the dilemma of allegiance to our heart and/or our family and society?

He is a tragic and romantic character all at once, and reminds us that no matter how many twists and turns life can take, or how many mistakes we make, the human spirit can overcome.

Further Character examples:

*Contemporary Examples:* **Thorin Oakenshield** (The Hobbit), **Peter Pettigrew** (Harry Potter), **Judy Moody** (Judy Moody series), **Darth Vader** (Star Wars), **Nancy Drew** (Nancy Drew Mysteries)

*Classic Examples:* **Emma** (Emma), **Dr. Jeykll & Mr. Hyde**, **Boo Radley** (To Kill a Mockingbird), **Stevens** (The Remains of the Day), **Tom Sawyer** (The Adventures of

Tom Sawyer), **Huck Finn** (The Adventures of Huckleberry Finn), **Headless Horseman** (Sleepy Hollow), **Jesus of Nazareth** (The Bible), **Jo March** (Little Women)

These are just a few examples of memorable characters in movie and literary history. Each of us are moved differently, but there are some consistent factors that make many of these characters stand out over others:

- Strong Spirit
- Empathy from reader
- A flaw

- Problem solving skills
- Relatable circumstance
- Fears

- Traits that remind readers of themselves
- Touches the dark places of our heart
- A sense of humor

So how do we develop memorable characters?

By creating characters our readers will believe in, and then making those characters strong. I would suggest doing this by:

- Strong character development

- Giving your characters real personalities

- Creating believable dialogue

Creating a character people will believe in takes time, but can be a lot of fun. The first step is strong character development.

# Character Development

A) Character Development = The creation of characters for a story.

B) Character Development = The evolution of a character within the story's framework.

The creation of characters for a story

Creating characters is one of the most fundamental pieces to creating a story. Many may find it easy to do, but others not so much. Here are some tips to keep in mind when creating characters for your story:

1.  Keep them real

2.  What makes them unique? What quirks do they have?

3.  Consider how others in the story will react to them

Keep Them Real

Readers will believe your character, admire your character, and fall in love with your character, if they believe your character is real. So give him/her a history, personality, passions, amusements, relationships, defects, ambitions – you get the point. Create your character to be a real person so they will leap off the page and into the hearts of your readers.

Providing a lineage and biography is unnecessary; inserting little snippets here and there is all it takes. Dropping a line about her being an orphan or being adopted is enough for the reader to make certain assumptions about the character's past and upbringing and reasons for current responses to certain situations. Hinting at an anger problem will cause your reader to wonder what will happen when a situation starts to escalate in the novel. Breadcrumbs are enough.

But keep in mind, you have created a world for your characters. Be sure your character is true to that world. If you've written a story taking place in the 1900's, your character can not be using 21$^{st}$ century words or slang.

What makes them unique? What quirks do they have?

We all want to be able to identify with the characters we read about. If they are perfect, they become stagnant. However, if your character is obsessed with pens and pencils and can't resist buying them every time she enters an office supply store, we'll that's something a little quirky and memorable – and potentially money draining. If your character voices their opinion each time someone irritates them, that could cause a ton of conflict and open up a lot of doors for your novel, and close many doors to solving the problem as well.

Developing idiosyncrasies, flaws, and unique traits for your character will help them become more memorable and give readers a chance to relate to them.

Consider how others in the story will react to them

The dynamics between characters is what keeps the story interesting. If you have an interesting and volatile character with no one to respond to his actions, the story is relatively dead. But if you have a cast of other characters all with their own unique personas, ready to respond in different ways to his actions, as well as each other's, you will have a variety of results which can move your story in countless directions.

So as you build each character, consider their role in the overall framework of the story. Sometimes you won't know. You may plan on them playing one role, but as the story develops, that particular character's place in it changes and they may become a more or less powerful force. Let the characters react to each other how they will and the story will become what it was meant to be.

## *The evolution of a character within the story's framework*

Character development, while incredibly important to the evolution of your story, is one of the most rewarding parts of writing. You have the opportunity to create a hero, a villain, and a cast of supporting characters each with the chance to become a better – or worse – person. They can of course stay the same person, but everyone is enchanted by a character who reminds them of themselves even in some small way, and changes.

As writers, it is our responsibility to create believable characters. Everyone goes about this differently – and I invite you to pursue all of the subjects in this book more thoroughly – but my philosophy on the matter is made up of three parts:

1.  Characters must be true to the world in which they are written

2.  Characters must have a flaw

3.  Characters must face a conflict and have the opportunity to make a change

I do not believe all characters have to be loved or liked, however you will have much better success if your main character is a person your readership likes to read about. So whether that means s/he is liked, respected, or simply empathized with, is up to you and your audience.

I personally feel my main character needs to be liked, have a flaw which readers can identify with, and my villain – while still a villain – is not *always* so horrible and bad, and sometimes has a flaw that readers can empathize or identify with. It makes for a more complex plot when rooting for the good guy isn't so black and white, and you have character development on both sides of the spectrum.

Character development can happen with all of your characters. It doesn't just need to happen with your protagonist (main good guy) and antagonist (main bad guy). In fact, I think it's important that it does – it provides more opportunity for conflict, tension, growth, and bonding.

The three points I addressed above have all been addressed briefly, but I will touch on them once again:

1. Characters must be true to the world in which they are written

   If your character suddenly starts talking like a scientist in the 1900's and he is a harpist in the 1800's, it's going to be very odd for the reader to believe in your character. It's important to be sure your character speaks, acts, and responds to his environment appropriately. Even if there is time-travel involved.

2. Characters must have a flaw

   As I've mentioned before, characters with flaws are believable and much more dynamic characters. Flaws give characters a chance to wonder or wish they were better at something or wish they didn't do something, and perhaps work throughout the story to improve on whatever that thing is. Or, to discover about themselves something we, as readers, already knew.

3. Characters must face a conflict and have the opportunity to make a change

Conflict is imperative because it's what the story is driving toward. It's what allows characters to change, or make life-changing decisions for themselves, or for the good – or ill – of many. This opportunity to face conflict is one both antagonists and protagonists should face. It tests our characters true nature and lays to rest any doubt readers may have about them.

Character development is great fun and you, as a writer, can go anywhere with it. I've often thought of it as the chance to become a variety of characters I would never actually be, but could explore to the maximum. And the best part, I can always write my own endings – and rewrite them if they didn't work out the way I wanted.

# Giving Your Characters Real Personalities

Beyond quirks and other character reactions, your main characters need to have real personalities. They don't necessarily have to be outgoing, dynamic, or outrageous, but they need to have depth.

If your protagonist is a CPA by day and gamer by night, enjoys Thai food and beer and that's all we know aside from he has suddenly become the suspect in a murder investigation – we might be intrigued in why he's a suspect and curious why the CPA/gamer combo, but other than that, nothing about him draws us in.

Now, if we know a little about his background – not a ton, just enough to start becoming emotionally involved – like he stops by the Thai place every night after work because that's where he and his girlfriend went before she died in a car accident – we might understand his obsession with Thai food a bit more. Or if we knew that he plays games religiously instead of pursuing a social life because that same girlfriend had encouraged him to chase after his dream of developing video games, we might understand the more you play, the more you learn. And he's not just playing, he's taking notes, observing, learning, and taking what he's learning and applying it to the new games he's developing. And not just any game – an action packed low violence game that he's hoping to be a massive hit; because he hates even the thought of shooting people - even on a video game.

So when he stops at the Thai place as usual but walks in during a robbery, he does what he can to help and is relieved when the robbers take off. So it comes as a shock when the police knock on his door and take him down to the precinct for questioning as their lead suspect in one of the robbers' murder.

Now, we are not only intrigued by what's happened, we've become more emotionally involved with our protagonist. We know he's a nice, gentle, hardworking guy, dependent on habit, who is trying to keep the dream of his girlfriend alive.

Giving your character personality involves small doses of personal history/background, a lot of showing (versus telling), obstacles to overcome so they can show their character, and other characters to interact with – giving your character the opportunity to display interpersonal skills.

Some great ways to provide your characters opportunities to demonstrate personality and character:

- Create obstacles for him to overcome

- Create an internal conflict for him to work through throughout the story

- Give him a flaw or two

- Allow him to suffer an injustice

- Put him or a loved one in danger

# Believable Dialogue

You know you've written great dialogue when your readers don't realize they're reading it. We've all been there: so consumed by a story, that we see and hear the character talking rather than see that they are lines on a page. That is how dialogue should be written.

So how do you do it?

There are a few steps to run your dialogue through to be sure your readers will believe your characters belong.

1. Keep your dialogue consistent with the personality of your character

2. Emulate the key components of real conversations

3. Use dialogue tags as appropriate

4. Have dialogue move your story forward; through action or thought

5. Limit your use of adverbs (good for all aspects of writing)

6. Read your dialogue out loud (good for all aspects of writing)

7. Practice writing the same scene from a different characters point of view

## **<u>Keep your dialogue consistent with the personality of your character</u>**

Every character in your story is created with a different personality. One of the best ways we show personality in writing is through dialogue.

Are they kind and gentle, or rough and mean? You can show this in how they speak and treat others.

Is your character an introvert but a genius, or an extrovert who is insecure? This can be shown in how much they speak, to whom, and what they say.

What country are they from (*accent*)? What region (*dialect*)? Are they religious (*habits they might refer to/attend to*)? Educated (*words they use*)?

Tons of options and all can be hinted at through dialogue.

With some many different types of personalities, it's important to be sure you keep your characters consistent throughout your story. As you review your book, short, excerpt, etc., it is imperative you match the correct character with the correct dialogue. If you don't know and believe in your characters, why should your reader?

## Emulate the key components of real conversations

How we actually speak can be boring. Next time you think about it, listen in on a conversation and think about what that might *read* like. So, we need to take the key components of real conversation and turn them into something that moves with our stories.

Take the action pieces, the story pieces, and the pieces of conversation that serve a purpose and include those in your dialogue. If it doesn't move it doesn't belong.

It's the same idea of using 'It is' versus 'it's.' 'It is' is technically the more grammatically correct way or proper way, but 'it's' is easier to say, read, and type.

Go with what your character would say. What would *you* say? It doesn't always have to be 'proper' but it does have to be real to your character. If not, the dialogue will be forced and awkward to write and read.

## Use dialogue tags as appropriate

What are dialogue tags? Things like 'he said' 'she added, then laughed' 'he whispered.' Tags note who said what with a little description on how they said it.

Be careful on what descriptive words you use as your tag. For example, you would not be able to say "'You are so funny,' she laughed." because a person can't laugh words. They'd have to say the words and laugh. Or laugh, say the words, and continuing laughing. You'd be better off with, "'You are so funny,' she said laughing." It's a technicality, and most everyone reading will know what you mean, but it's one an editor will get you on.

On this same note of tags, use them as appropriate and feel free to include names of other characters in dialogue that another character is addressing, either verbally, with thought, or with an action. You don't need to use them every time someone speaks. If you only have two speakers, your reader should be able to follow along well enough to know who is who, with the occasional tag.

When you get three or more speakers, it's better to add more tags, or more names being addressed. But again, tags are not needed after every statement. Good rule of thumb: read your dialogue out loud to someone not related to your story and see if they can follow along. Or, have them read it.

## Have dialogue move your story forward; through action or thought

Writing dialogue can be challenging. But keep in mind, the goal of dialogue in your story isn't to establish pleasantries or talk about our day like we would in person, it's to move the story forward and provide insight.

While it's perfectly normal for us to chatter away in real life, in stories, that sort of back-and-forth is distracting, can bore your reader, and rarely occurs in good writing. Your reader is unaccustomed to it and while they may not know exactly what the problem is, they'll know something is off with the dialogue.

If your characters don't have a point – if they don't have a reason they are speaking to help move the story forward – they shouldn't be speaking at all.


**Here's an example:**

Alice jumped for the phone on the first ring.

"Hello?"

"Hi Alice, it's Mary."

"Hi Mary. What's up?"

"Oh, nothing. Just thought I'd call and say hi. What are you up to?"

"Just the same stuff. Hanging out at home, watching TV, and waiting for Jason to call. Nothing new."

Mary laughed. "Yeah, I guess not! By the way, I actually did see Jason at the mall earlier."

"What? What was he doing there?"

"I don't know. But he was with a bunch of people I didn't know. That's why I didn't see him at first. There was also some redhead hanging all over him…"

Alice continued to listen and realized this was the *real* reason Mary called. How could she call Mary her best friend when she constantly toyed with her like this?

This is all something we would say in a real-life situation, however on the page it's a bit painful because the point - the action – doesn't happen until line six. Then the tension picks up and we discover the true nature of Alice and Mary's friendship.

Here's another way to approach the same scenario:

Alice stared blankly at the TV screen. Another mundane Saturday. The ringing phone brought her to life and she snatched it up on the first ring.

"Hello?"

"Alice, it's Mary! You will *never* guess who I saw at the mall yesterday."

*Oh no,* thought Alice. *What is she going to torture me with now?* Her thoughts immediately went to her boyfriend Jason, whose silence lately had caused her to wonder exactly where they stood.

"Okay I'll just tell you since you're thinking too much, *as usual.* Jason!"

Alice's heart plummeted. "We'll you don't have to sound happy about it, Mary."

"And there was a gorgeous red-head hanging all over him. So, where were you?"

Hopefully you find the second example more engaging and see how dialogue can not only inform, but move the story along.

## **Limit your use of adverbs (good for all aspects of writing)**

Adverbs, as a general rule, tend to detract from the strength of your dialogue. They are good words, but writers have traditionally depended on them too much to convey the meaning they are hoping their dialogue is already doing. Adverbs are oftentimes unneeded. An action or a description could be used in its place.

Simply take a look at where you've placed an adverb to see if it is helping or hindering your dialogue and if an action or description would be better suited in its place.

Here's a quick example:

*Sentence using adverb:*

"Well now that's a good idea isn't it?" he said <u>sarcastically</u>.

*Sentences using description in place of an adverb:*

"Well now that's a good idea isn't it?" he said rolling his eyes and using his John Wayne voice.


## **Read your dialogue aloud (good for all aspects of writing)**

I'm a proponent of reading all writing aloud. It does wonders for discovering inconsistencies, odd phrases, and hiccups in pacing. It's also great for hearing where your dialogue runs a little dry or feels awkward. You really don't know what you're writing sounds like unless you hear it. If you only read it, your mind easily inserts how it should sound.

## Practice writing the same scene from a different characters point of view

This of course is not mandatory, but I encourage you to consider this exercise. Writing the same scene from a variety of points of view or character perspectives gives you the opportunity to determine whether or not you've selected the correct character to voice it.

It also helps you get to know your characters on a more intimate level and allows them to speak to you. Sometimes, all our characters need is the opportunity to share and they'll tell us what we need to know to move our story in the right direction.

Dialogue can be one of the most difficult things to write, but it's crucial to weaving your story together. The better you know your characters – their quirks, faults, redeeming features, what makes them laugh, what makes them cry – the more you can convey their personalities through their everyday speech. And the more believable your dialogue will be.

# Character Development Exercises

<u>ONE</u>

Write a list of all the characters in your story.

On a separate page for each character, write out a character sketch including:

- Name
- Age
- Gender
- Physical description
- Family history
- Physical location (past, present)
- Likes, dislikes
- Favorite activities
- Most memorable experience

<u>TWO</u>

Identify two – five of your main characters.

After you've done the above character sketch, identify the flaws for each of these characters.

Then, consider where you'd like these characters to be by the end of the story. They don't have to end up here since we know writing doesn't always end the way we think it will - but for now, jot something down.

If you can, write down a few events that may help them get to this point. If that's too much planning, that's okay! We don't all work with outlines.

Hang onto this – see where your characters end up at when your story is complete.

### THREE

Write one scene involving your protagonist where s/he:

- Faces a fear

- Reflects on where they live

- Remembers something that happened in the past

- Wonders how they will overcome _____

- Muses on how they feel about another person in the story

# Character Personality Exercises

Write a paragraph or two where you describe how your character acts/responds when you:

- Create obstacles for him to overcome

- Create an internal conflict for him to work through throughout the story

- Give him a flaw or two

- Allow him to suffer an injustice

- Put him or a loved one in danger

You can create hypothetical scenarios based upon his actual character, or situations that are actually occurring in your story so you may use them later in your finished product.

# Dialogue Exercises

Below are exercises you can work on for each component we addressed earlier as you move forward with your writing. These simple exercises are meant to help get ideas flowing and give you an opportunity to implement ideas you may have had while reading.

## Keep your dialogue consistent with the personality of your character

Does your character have an accent, or is of a particular age where they speak slightly different than other characters in your story? Many of our characters talk in a specific fashion unique to them. If not with accents or dialects, with use of certain words or with certain attitudes.

Review your characters' speech to be sure it remains consistent throughout your story. You don't want your high school educated French gypsy to sound like a PhD from Scotland by the end of the story.

If you need help keeping your characters straight, map them out on paper, or highlight them in different colors on your computer with a color key code.

## Emulate the key components of real conversations

As an experiment, record yourself and a willing friend conversing normally. Take that short conversation and cut out the unnecessary pieces so you get to the meat of the conversation. Then, edit what you've kept to the voice of your character.

## Use dialogue tags as appropriate

As you re-read your story, check to be sure your speakers are clear. This is most easily done if you read the story aloud, or have another person read the story.

When you check for adverbs and read the story aloud, you can also check to be sure your dialogue tags are in place. Experiment with removing, replacing, rewording, and rearranging the tags to find the best use of tags and the smoothest transitions.

## Have dialogue move your story forward; through action or thought

Write a scene including a good portion of dialogue, just as it comes to your mind. Don't worry about using tags or showing action – just get the bones on the page.

Go back and rewrite the scene focusing first on how you can use action to move to story forward, then again focusing on thought.

Once both have been written, see what you can pull from all three to make your final piece of writing full of action, thought, and description to create the ideal scene.

## Limit your use of adverbs (good for all aspects of writing)

Select a section of your story you've already written you'd like to work on. Once printed, go through and circle all the words ending in '-ly.' As a general rule, adverbs generally end in '-ly.' Once completed, see which of these words can either be:

- Eliminated

- Changed to an action word

- Changed to a description word

Which of the above options will make your writing stronger and covey the meaning of your dialogue best? Sometimes the adverb *is* the best option, and that's okay! But it's a good idea to review the number of adverbs you are using and if they are the words that can do the best job in that particular place.

## Read your dialogue aloud (good for all aspects of writing)

In this exercise, simply read portions of your story aloud. It may be helpful to read it to someone else to have that extra pair of ears listening, but do what you are comfortable with. It is important to at least read it to yourself – I can guarantee you will hear something that you'll want to tweak.

## Practice writing the same scene from a different characters point of view

This exercise gives you practice in seeing and voicing the same scene from a variety of characters' point of view. It is a great exercise to help you familiarize yourself with all your characters and prepare yourself for how they will react to future situations. Even if you don't use all the scenes you write, they are beneficial to both you, your characters, and your story as you will all evolve and grow together into a more cohesive unit.

# Meet the Author

I'm Joy Burke. I'm a freelance writer and developmental editor in Washington state and author of *A Book of Shorts: Stories from Various Drawers.* Creative writing has been my first love for over 25 years. I have been a freelance professional business writer since 2012 with clients including Gilpin Real Estate, King Enterprises, and Everett Chiropractic Center. As I transition into Northwest Women Writers Coordinator, I have also shifted my focus to helping aspiring writers reach their full potential by bringing Haha! Ink! Creative Studios front and center.

I look forward to working with authors from all walks of life and at every stage of the journey.

Here's to your success and creativity!

# Let's Connect

I hope you've enjoyed *Fundamentals of Creative Writing* and have found some useful tidbits you can start applying right away.

If you are interested in learning more, have questions, or have a manuscript you'd like to work on, please let me know. I'd love to work with you!

You can find me online at:

Website: www.hahaink.com

Twitter: @joyaburke

LinkedIn: linkedin.com/in/joyaburke

Email: contact@hahaink.com

***Happy Writing!***

# Also By Joy...

## A Book of Shorts:
*Stories from Various Drawers*

## Fundamentals of Creative Writing:
*Building the Foundations of a Real World*

## Picking Up:
*A Book of Story <u>Starts</u>*

# *Coming Soon!*

## The GREAT[SM] Principle
*Content Marketing made Easy*

www.ingramcontent.com/pod-product-compliance
Lightning Source LLC
Chambersburg PA
CBHW070459290526
45790CB00003B/1026